# UNEARTHINGS

# WENDY CHEN

TAVERN BOOKS

PORTLAND

Printed in the United States of America.

Cover art: Wendy Chen, *Untitled,* 2017. Pastel on paper.
Copyright © Wendy Chen. Courtesy of the artist.

Chen, Wendy 1992 -

ISBN-13: 978-1-935635-80-2 (paperback)
ISBN-13: 978-1-935635-81-9 (hardcover)

LCCN: 2017963625

FIRST EDITION

98765432 First Printing

TAVERN BOOKS
Union Station
800 NW 6th Avenue #255
Portland, Oregon 97209
www.tavernbooks.org

# Table of Contents

*for my family*

# All Their Awful Particles

I am calling up the dead—the dead of my family.
I pull them out of the earth by their hair, by the fistful.
I scrutinize their bodies, green as acid, for traces of mine.

How can I stop looking at them?
At their faces?

Their lives pour into me through a silver faucet
I cannot turn off. Their deaths, too—

suicide, suicide:
the familial sickness.

Surely it has congealed within me—
all their awful particles.

If I were the firstborn, mystical or clean
like a sheet of cotton twisting in the wind—

No.

I am a piece of slate stained,

scarred with footprints of the dead.

Are they confessing what they've done
to make me?

They lay their hands on me
like strips of seaweed.

When I place my mouth at my feet,
unable to speak,
I feel their malformed sadness comb through my hair.

# They Sail Across the Mirrored Sea

*Ascending, wheeling*
*in a gyre, the roc*
*spreads his wings*
*ninety thousand li.*
*Bearing the blue sky,*
*he looks down, surveying*
*the little kingdoms of Man.*

—Mao Zedong, "Dialogue Between Birds"

1.

Grandma always spoke fondly of the shrimp
in the spring at the edge of the village.
No bigger than her smallest finger, they frothed
in the pool—rice-paper shells
bandaged around a bit of milky gray.

Small vehicles of life in deadwater.
They moved like a great fleet of dragon boats
from one end of the spring to another,

their legs the oars of many men.

For them, the spring was a lake—
an ocean—a continent of water. It was all

they needed to survive. There was nothing else,
no food for them to feed on.
They sprouted from the rock itself—
a deep pact between stone and water.

And what did they think of her small net?

A fibrous constellation pulled out of the sky,
descending, penetrating the defenseless water with ease,
carrying them toward the edge.

The constant pressure of water—suddenly gone:
a strange lightness unbearable.

Were they aware of body, and not-body?
of mind, and not-mind? In the air,
blind as they had ever been.

How crisp they tasted fresh out of the water!
They tasted even better in the wok: lotus-leaf

shells blooming like rust under oil and tender iron.

Was the water dark or full of light?

At times, the spring glowed, thinking itself
an ocean and its inhabitants
phosphorous beings.


2. (1967)

The fields heaved like a fur-thickened hide
under the midday sun. Men and women
labored in its deep folds.

Ma was upset again, the sadness
shining from her face like liquid
moonlight poured over the earth.

The badge-wearing children had come knocking at the door
again, demanding all their photographs. The colored one, too. Yes,
even the colored one had been scratched up and taken away to the fire.

It was no use consoling her—
She was inconsolable.

It was so expensive, she said.
You looked so pretty in your new dress, she said.
And the one with your grandmother—
the last one I had.

Uncle came from the city to visit, decorated
and uniformed, bringing with him
coupons for extra portions of rice and cotton.

Even that was not enough to make her smile.

Sister, he said, pull back your dark-gray hood. These things are not
necessary for life or for happiness. And the wok, too. The wok must go.
Our soldiers need the iron. Our fields have sprouted out of their blood.
Our fences stacked with their bones. There are certain rivers here,
crossing the land like polluted veins, filled with the piss of dead men.

Sister, he said, I have journeyed through the primal world and seen
what evil crouches over small huts. Establish your mind on the highest
cliff, where the eagle's nest dwells. Bring your feet to the precipice, and
you will see the birds who turn from wing to wing.

Even that was not enough to make her smile.

3. (1944)

Late summer brought the cooling of bamboo mats,
and the Japanese soldiers.

It was said they came from Beijing where
the river dolphins played in the Yangzi.

What did they know of the war,
living, as they did, underwater?
Did they taste the bodies that sugared
the banks with blood? Did bullets pass
dripping brightfire through the water?

She had been warned often of what they could do,
what they had done in Nanjing:
bayoneted women in their full-moon bellies,
forced fathers to fuck their daughters,
and afterwards taken photographs—
little trophies to remember the war by.

> *Ba, but they look like us.*
> *Pale-skinned and dark-eyed,*
> *with long, straight hair like the fibers*
> *of falling stars.*

*No, my daughter, they are not like us,*
*not like us at all, these* ri ben gui.
*They sail across the mirrored sea*
*with blood on their flags*
*and minds.*

On the day they first came,
the stew on the fire was boiling,
boiling and boiling.

For three weeks, the meat had fallen
away from the pig in long, fibrous strips
and now its bones turned, uneasy,
in the pot.

Ma was sucking on a thick, yellow bone, sucking out
its spongy stuff.

There's always something left for you
to eat, she said,
even when all the meat is gone.

She lapped at the bone with a little pink tongue.

In the distance came the sound

of the alarm,
a long wail, passing
like a ghost through the village.

Bare feet, river hair.

Ma tugged her to her feet. Their small bones
gathered themselves quickly, running
toward the cover of the forest. Near the edge,
she turned and looked through rows of bamboo,
toward the village where the slow ones began to
fall. Her stomach growled.

She thought sadly of the soup left on the table.

In the spring, the shrimp continued to swim.
To them, it was a quiet evening: distilled with light
passing on its way through the universe.

# Memorial

Li Qingzhao wrote under the name of Yi'an,
which means "the dweller
who is easily at peace."

"...at every snowstorm,
Yi'an would put on her bamboo hat and cloak of reeds
and go out on top of the city walls,
looking into the distance..."

Lately, I've been translating her poems,
though in dreams she comes untranslated:
cape of reeds, cap of snow.
The snow falls like a net of spiders
across her back and her face
has wandered off.
Only her clothes, empty of a body,
stumble across the winter scene.

Yi'an,
it has been almost a thousand years
since you last walked on top of the city wall.
Still, I follow you, doggedly,

like a child in a story.
And each year the snow melts on my face
the same way it did yours.

# It is a house

I shared one face with the family
it had been painted had been made up like a house
it had one maternal eye one paternal eye
each was glassy as a window
the nose a door no mouth

and so for all those years I didn't speak
said nothing even when they put me in the chair
they peered down into me from such a height their eyes were large
they wanted me to talk I knew but didn't
I learned silence kept us safe

but speaking now I've lost all face I've cast it off
parted I stand outside
I pace up and down the walkway
press my mouth against the drag of heels on stone
can I enter still or must I leave
the house makes no reply its silence is

the moon is empty of the rabbit and the girl
even they are ashamed of what I have done
now it is dark

the windows fill with lights one by one
can I make myself a new face if I have none

# Fastened I

I wouldn't speak to you
when I was angry.

You told me you'd die
without my love.

That summer, you tried.
In the hospital room,

your little sister
wouldn't touch your hand.

Your mother kept fixing
her gaze to your feet

and the nurses came and went
wielding pitched voices.

Three weeks later,
you called again.

In your message, you spoke

distantly,
telling me how pale

the curtains were, yellow, hanging
against the walls.

The plastic vase on the table was a stony
kind of blue.

And the television,
switching through faces,
was bolted to the floor.

# Imago

Madame Butterfly doesn't know why
she wakes this way.

By now, half
her body

is grafted
with silk,

each thread
a ligature.

Madame Butterfly should be pleased
with the work,

but her face
is growing paler

and paler.
Soon, it will be

pale and flat

as the moon.

Lunar beauty.
Alien.

Madame Butterfly should be
grateful

that others
find her pleasing.

Madame Butterfly is
grateful.

She was made
to please.

Her natural lifespan is spent
passing

among the cherry trees,
kneeling down in snow.

Madame Butterfly knows
her body

is a doorway.
A moon gate.

A trail
of white jasmine.

Bound by her dark
cocoon,

she blinks her one
remaining eye.

# Strawberries

Cretan coastline: a shimmering
blue siren. The cornsilk light.
Dog's tooth white.

Father, Mother,
it was a good day,
passing like a strip of film.

His hand in her hair.
His mouth to her ear.

I followed behind
with a pint of strawberries.

Coming back
up the mountain,
sliding on the slope,
I stumbled at the edge
of the temporary door.

The strawberries
spilled across the painted floor.

They were falling down the hill.

Enough
to summon his anger kept
at bay for an hour, two days.

I left,
the rest of me after
my blown-away face.

Years later, Mother you were still
picking up strawberries from the ground.
They clotted your nails. Your hands, your mouth

were red. Your eyes.

# August 18th

From the summer porch,
I watch

the night-blooming
cereus.

Its flowering
past the hour.

O, maternal voice,
paternal voice—

their laughter
through the screen.

Smell of bread,
still warm, being broken.

# No use to say

that I was born here
in a small red house
on the Connecticut River.

In winter, we'd walk
by its strip of Listerine
blue ice,

knowing spring
would turn our prints
to water,

and water
to New England clay.

No. I am not
American.
For you, I am

from no country
but the East,
my body fragrant
as star anise.

# The Encounter

She is not a body,
not at all.

Just a doorway.

If you raise her face
to yours,

you can see through,
underneath.

And just beyond—

fragrant twists of smoke and
placid thighs.

This red blossom
is her mouth.

It only speaks
your name.

You know yourself
against her.

Your maleness,
whiteness

thrown into relief.

Whole, at last,
and prime.

You leave her
empty.

Draw over
her dead body a silk curtain

embroidered with smiling cranes.

# Fastened II

You told me your father had hurt you
that evening in the hotel
overlooking the harbor.

You left without your jacket.
Your face scraped
against the wind.

The water was green. It was blue.
And down on the street,
by the boardwalk,
lights were coming on again.

People
were getting into their cars.
Yes, they were going on.

Hours, you walked around the city.
Boston was quiet in the evenings.
It was green. It was blue.

You had spent your childhood in loud cities,

streets spilled over with people.

Here, it was nearly empty.
The avenues bare
as you.

You wanted to forget.
You told me to remember.

Impassable day
you passed through.

# They Call Me Madame Butterfly

My skin is as thin
as rice paper
stretched across a frame.

My lips as red
as a temple door.

I am not like other women.

I won't walk,
won't talk
without you.

I'll wait
in a field of snow,
listening for the click
of your heels on ice,
for your black leather shoes.

When your hands
touch my cheeks—

I'll blossom
like a cherry tree.

Mouthless

flower
in the snow,

I'll raise my head.
I'll fix my eyes on you.

Won't you recognize me?
You know you do.

You were the one
wearing my voice,
making incisions
inside me.

How blank the interior!
How perfectly smooth.
Pale as the lining of a clam.

But you grow tired
of inhabiting me: retreat,

retreat from my pink
lacquered shell.

# Psalms

In sculpture, we make the body before the face.

When my mother met my father, she thought she would conceive by holding hands.

In *Journey to the West*, a monkey is born from stone.

My teacher asks me to sculpt the hands again. I start over, smoothing down the thumb and knuckle. Clay folds into clay.

On the television, Buddha traps the stone monkey in his palm. His hand is large as the heavens.

I look into the mirror at my own hands, placed at different angles on my body.

The girl I love tells me how her father reaches under her clothes. When she takes my picture, her eyes like a hand trace the curves of my face.

When I leave her, she wraps her arms around her body as if it might leap away.

I scroll images of hands online. Renaissance shades. Post-modern wires. Digital skin.

A glazed, white statuette of Guanyin, the goddess of mercy, stands on my parent's bureau. One hand holds a willow branch, the other faces outward. Her fingers are slender and smooth, jointless.

I study the inside. Count the bones. The hand is like the foot, each finger a toe.

In Beijing, there were no taxis in the street. Father carried me on his back to the hospital, his hands clasping my arms.

He has kept journals since he was young.

I look to Rodin's hands for guidance. *Fording the Stream. Exhortation. The Kiss.*

The boy who loves me tells me I am his. When he holds me, he curls his arms around my neck.

In my father's hand, there is the hand of his father. In mine too, he is there.

I was taught the face was more important than the hand. The face belongs to the family. It can be lost and never regained. But they said nothing about the hand.

My teacher's hands carved the same block of granite for years. It stood outside his kitchen window, weathering over time into the face of a woman.

Camille Claudel sculpted many of the hands and feet in Rodin's sculptures. The hand of a woman has no name.

The priest tells Mother she was born an earth rat. The lines in her palm promise a life of labor.

I spray down the clay on the armature with water and wrap it in plastic. At night, the studio is filled with shrouded arms, shoulders, cheeks.

Grandma used to walk with me outside the house. Now, the veins in her arm are too small to find. The nurses draw blood from the back of her hand.

I hold my fingers up to the light. I learn the shadows of my palms. When I was young, Grandma called them pianist hands.

My mother likes to tell her family I am a writer, a *zhou jia*. *Zhou* for making. *Jia* for house, and also family.

I climb the mountain. In the temple, Guanyin is carved out of the red
rock. On either side of her, a child. Their hands are clasped in prayer.

My cousin cut her hair to become the boy her father always wanted.

My hair has always been long. Father used to dry mine, sifting through
each strand.

A poet is a *shi ren*, a poem-person.

Shamefully, I unearth the dead, our secrets.

At times, I want my hand to be nameless, but it has a face.

The monkey made of stone walks fourteen years on foot to be
awakened. He wears Guanyin's divine circlet.

I walk through the woods with Mother and Father. Light on the rocks.
Sometimes, they clasp hands.

I stopped sculpting bodies in clay long before I learned to sculpt hands.

After hours of chiseling stone, the hands turn stiff, paralyzed. From
working clay, the ache is deeper, unfinished:

another hand is still growing in mine.

# Madame Butterfly at the Auction House

Here is her torso.

It opens up
like a refrigerator.

Inside,

see how neatly her organs are arranged
on built-in plastic shelving.

Her real mouth also is here.

We sealed it away,
in a deep jar.

It was ugly. A coiling proboscis
in the brine.

Nothing

at all like her slender,
chambered heart,

which is industrial red,
auto gloss,

the size of a toy
in your hand.

If you knock it
against table legs, stair landings—

If you give it to your children
to play with—

it will light up
like a wand.

# No More Cows

Sitting down wordlessly
in a landscape free of cows.

We spend the week looking for them,
for their crude flame.

Suddenly a month
and still no cows.

A sense of relief, yes
the last one we saw was the last.

Now, we draw signs of our affection
in the sand.

Your mouth traces
my hand.

And just when we begin
to love one another again,

there is one

coming toward us, two, three,

a herd,
their clamorous patchiness

looking as if God had pressed
his muddy palms all over.

Looking at us
with their primary eyes.

All their silence
hinging on ours.

# In Which I Am Afflicted with Mme. Butterfly

If only it were so easy
to root her out

like a bit of decay in the heart
of a molar.

But no, I feel her pulsing
in the crook

of my elbow:
a worm in the blood.

It was always easier
—safer—

to take her
into me:

her passivity, her silence
into mine.

I have grown up

with her inside me:

larval,
then larger.

Now, we are
cheek to cheek,

her mouth
to mine.

No way to cut her out,
pull her out

through my throat.
If I could, I would

part us
piece by piece:

wing from shoulder,
proboscis from tongue.

Lay the two of us out
on a table: Madame Butterfly
and I.

# Animal Whiteness

Walking with you
between the birches—

their animal whiteness,
slender innocence.

The trailhead
washed green,
lit with rain.

Evening coming in
a few miles away.

Father, you carried me over
the flooded bridge.

My arms, still young,
around your neck.

# Ordinary Clamor

MOTHER half-hidden under the blankets of her bed.
FATHER downstairs, in the basement. SISTER outside
talking to the cop on the porch, talking
and not-talking with her stickered-on mouth.

It is a doll's house, bisected
anatomical model: the kitchen
cut straight down, the granite split
in two. Even the water that drips
from the faucet is only half a drop.

When I look again, Mother has disappeared,

is hiding
in the corner, quiet
as a lamp.

Only her naked feet are revealed to me
beneath the dark, velvet curtains.

✶

Father, father—

His anger comes and goes.

His happiness is light
moving across
the milk on the table
in an old painting.

✳

Mother says I remember only
what should be forgotten.

But I remember
the sweetness too—
the way he'd clean my bike...

O muddy wheel turning in air, o soft
blue rags.

✲

There were days
when the plates
remained whole.
Their wholeness held
light like water.

✳

In June, Father cut down
the blue plastic birds
Mother hung.

Their wire strings
dangled
from the branches.

I stood
mute as a stillborn.

\*

Father, father—

Father's father did not spare his hand.
He loved his sons. His daughters
not at all.

I think—though I have never
seen him—I can see
Grandfather
in Father's face.

Father can be patient,
most
with me.

He says *Your tears are the only*
He says *You are not like her*

Mother always sent me
to make peace.

✳

While words burned
inside Sister's throat.

Scorch marks formed
along her cheek.

*

Still Mother did not leave,
not even after that day
in June.

Inside, our voices had been blown out
to an awful pitch.

Through the window, I saw
the birds leave
with their
ordinary clamor.

✳

I am my Father,
as he is his.

At times I want us torn
and torn until the pieces
are too small to love.

✳

Beside you in bed
for thirty years,
Mother, it was just
a bristling armful of
blue flames.

✳

Mother says, *Stay, for love.*

While I,
I think I would die...

✳

This is where we learned to ride our bikes,
lie down
and draw around our bodies with chalk.

Every year, the children
of the neighborhood still
dig through the snow
at the end of the road.

And when it is warm again,
in light, in spring,
they stand in circles holding hands.

✷

Sister, if there are birds again,
let them be small as ash
and full of mouths.

They will feed on my words,
and carry them away.

Mother, unyoke yourself
from your lethal cart of sorrow.

Put down the hammer, Father.
Lower your hand.

Sister, let us cut these old strings
that have grown from us like hair.

# Translating Li Qingzhao

You, from outside, look in
past the bamboo screen
blue with night,
the sheer curtains
layer after layer,
to where she is sleeping
on top of the blankets,
furrowed, red as a peeled cherry,
to where she is waking—

waking, sitting up
on the bed, walking
sitting again in the chair,
shining like a mineral
in the candlelight,
the fertile gleam
of her eyes, her hair
still bound up
in its nautilus curls,

letting each one down now,
plucking out the gatherings

of the day, the long stretch of year:
the cold twigs collected
from the glossy banks of the river,
the drunken flowers
from underneath
the eastern fence,
the scorching voices of the geese
as they leave.

Always, she thinks,
always, the geese are leaving.

See how she arranges them,
on the table,
their little vowels.
Her fingers, precise as scalpels.
The fine hairs on her knuckles,
swept forward,
like yours.

Uncork the bottle of wine by the elbow,
sweet rice wine, sweet and cloudy,
pouring out from mouth to mouth.

# Fastened III

Inside, there was
a nocturnal well:
a bed you slept in.

It was white, veinless.
And the long sheet
curled around me.
It was like your arm,
like you.

You kept
on the table
the necklace of your father:
a chain of beads:
scarred quartz.

# Ghost-catcher

Tonight, I've brought you with me
here into the water
to catch our ghosts, collect
our lives from the dead.

Daughter, don't be afraid.

They float around us belly up,
like clouds of flour
thrown into the water,
nudging against our knees,
germinating faces, beastly
and familiar.

There goes the arm of a grandmother.

A brother's ankle. A twin's cheek.
Hardly stir them with a finger
and they break apart, elusive
wisps, stringy and genetic.
Impossible to sift through them all.

Pull one up by its unbound hair.

That is your great-grandfather, coiling
round us like the rope
that wound around his neck.
Father always said it was his death
that saved him, called back home
for his funeral that day
instead of being sent to Vietnam.

We must have been there with him,
swinging in the dust underneath his feet.

# Li Qingzhao on the Subject of Loneliness

When he was away from me,
when he was traveling, a stranger
on the roads
to other cities—

All day long, I sat beside the window with the paper curtain.
I would lean over the jade railing.

Below, in the courtyard,
where he liked to walk,
the feather of a passing goose.

Was he crossing over water cold as zinc?
Was he passing under the lintel?

For weeks, I wondered. All
those years, and after
finding him in that last inn,
the same.

And lost. And I lost

all those things we kept:
the vase, green as parsley,
the ivory hog,
the words cut in stone.

At night when I wake,
the places they once occupied in my thoughts
gleam, the emptiness there bright as the paws of a sphinx,
filled, now, with me.

# Fastened IV

It was like you,
your love,
the kind of love they put in writing.

Your love it had eyes,
a throat,
two breasts, gummy and white,
even a voice.

In the night, I woke.

It was huddled in the corner,
watching us, wanting
to name itself,
to bind us foot to foot.

It was like a child,
so much like a child—
younger than a day.

It was the kind of love that makes you go back
and go back.

I never wanted that.

# A Dialogue on Fences

BUTTERFLY

Each year they drink down my death
as a libation.

They write and rewrite my body
for a theater whose doors
are barred against me.

I have lived through all their
resurrections.

It is not my life they want.
It is that final death scene.

They say they grace my life with tragedy.

Each time I wake they build another
chain link fence around me.

LI QINGZHAO

The aluminum hooves of the composers keep
stumbling over our bodies.

Tip out
your electric lantern
full of words.

# In Praise of Humiliations

they discuss at their conferences the dynamics of inequality
devote an hour a timeslot or two
their skin glows bluely white their teeth
we watch from our seats a distance

it will not be me could it be you
one among us placed in their histories
how could it be me be you
no name no face to put a name to

at night what I have felt nurses against me
woundedness shame minor humiliations
how I longed to have their hair their lives

now each year I cultivate my humiliations
pray they bud on me like the sprouts of an old potato
and while I sleep let me grow my eyes

# A Collector's Guide to the Preservation of *Lepidoptera*

Butterfly remains in the house of her husband. She waits for his return, refusing to marry again. She waits for him whom she loves without pause.

*The interior of the caterpillar is removed by carefully pressing it out.*

Three years pass and there is news of him again. Delighted, Butterfly prepares the house. She raises the curtains and washes their son's hair. This time he will stay.

*The butterflies themselves are simply dried with great care, pinned.*

In the middle of the night, Butterfly wakes. She hears the sound of his footsteps upon the streets of Nagasaki. He is reaching toward her—for his son in her arms.

*The specimens are mounted and covered with glass lids.*

She is not his, but she is his...

Puccini, give her the knife.

# Descent

In the courtyard,
they are burning

a paper house
and a paper car.

The ashes drift into the morning
of the fourth day.

Her body is laid out
on packets of dry ice, waiting

for all her sons
to return.

The priestesses say
their last blessings.

My father and his brother
bear their mother

down

twenty flights.

I follow with my aunts
in our long, white tunics.

Behind us,
the processional.

At the crematorium, we bow
turn by turn.

An hour, and we are
beckoned in.

On a steel tray,
ash

in the shape of a body
streaked through with bone.

Father
breaks down

the skull
into smaller pieces.

On the outskirts of the city, we file
up a steep hill.

The family tomb
cut into the hillside

has been opened
for our arrival.

As Father places her urn
among them,

Uncle says, "Foreign child,
you too

have a place here."

# Fastened V

Weeks again of patient blues.

You folded down
into yourself.

You could bear no voice,
no face
but your own.

Not even mine,
which you said you loved.

The old films you watched without sleep,
you muted.

You looked from a distance
at figures on the screen:

two lovers
beneath the tracks
just standing apart, entirely themselves
like figures undersea.

Salt gathered on their faces...

And then the days
you leapt out of widening
doors, from passageways, taking me
by the hand outside.

It was a new world.
It had an astral underside.
It was starry all over.
You were something very young.

That night, I stood in the kitchen
with its ticking faucet.
You slept
in your boatful of dreams.

Water kept coming in,
going out,
leaving me alone
with the voice of my mother.

Old kernel of a voice.
It was saying *Stay, for love.*
It was saying *Love, stay.*

# The Ghosts

1.

When the soldiers begin to rape Nanjing, his father
orders his wives to pack up the silver.

They'll send it all
to the family estates outside Yangzhou
where *nai nai* and *ye ye* live.

The boy watches his mother kneel
by the wooden crates,
lining them with silk to muffle
the ingots on their journey out of the city—

miles and miles
in lacquered carriages, rolling
over threads of packed dirt that lead
to the countryside.

How many men are needed
to unload the crates? How long
will they remember the savage

weight in their arms? What treasure
must they be carrying into the wild fields?

They dig a small grave
for each one and swear
on their ghosts to forget
what they've buried, and where.


2.


When the Japanese are driven off,
the civil war resumes
and leather-faced bandits roam
the land with Soviet guns.

      Mad Dog comes across
      a red-tiled manor, empty
      but for an old man
      and his hobbled bitch. He hates
      the pale women with hooved feet
      who think they are too good
      to walk this earth.

      He takes them both outside

to kill or to ransom...
while he decides, his men
are loosed upon the grounds.

One comes running back, shouting
that he's found houses, houses
full of grain. Rice and wheat and
other drystuff, enough to feed them all
for months.

Mad Dog orders his men to empty
the carts of loot and fill them all with grain
instead, more precious than gold or silver
which you cannot eat or drink.

He knows how it is to starve,
to wish you could eat your own body.

3.

*Nai nai* dies in the winter
and *ye ye* in the spring.

His father buries them

in a plot with the other mothers
and fathers and sisters and brothers.

The boy kneels before them all
while stone beasts look on
with ancestral eyes.

Smoke rises
from sticks of sandalwood to join
the vaporous pollutions of
a country, burning.


4.


*How long you wander*
*the field, the grainhouses. Now*
*all's empty—*
*the manor, picked over.*

*You watch them cart away*
*the cypress chairs, the hanging*
*scrolls, the mother-of-pearl*
*music box.*

*No one visits*
*to remind you of your name*
*as your body splits*
*under earth.*

*The sight*
*drives you away to the fields*
*tipped with straws of rice.*

*You watch the dew*
*on blades, the lazy suspension*
*of winged-things.*

*When the wind picks up*
*before the rain, it lifts*
*the honeyed scent of bodies*
*digested by the earth.*

*Smell the dust and forget*
*you ever had a body at all.*


5.


Eventually, they come:
the ones who have heard

of the silver buried on the family estate.

They pick a clear, birdless day and start
by the ransacked manor,
bringing with them buckets of water
they tip carefully over the soil, watching...

Beside them, the ghosts watch
too, pulling at their muddy ankles.

They curse the living who come
with eyes that shine like coins—

for where the water sinks the fastest,
there will be treasure.

# Rites

Grandma wondered as I cut her hair
if I would mourn her when she died.

On the television, a discordant chorus
of weeping girls
crowded around a white,
maternal sheet.

She doesn't believe in the afterlife,
only the proper rites.

Mother thinks we will be born again.
She does not wish to linger
in ceremonies, the grave.
She says that we will
meet again.

But Yama, receiving souls of the dead
in his judgment hall,
says we must forget
our past lives.

He measures out
the punishment that is our due:
twenty, forty, maybe
a hundred years
of weeping
is needed before we can be
colorless and new.

Grandma emerges from the shower.
By now the girls have quieted. A man
is selling scissors.

I dry her with the towel. First her hair,
dove grey with strands of white.
Her neck, her shoulders and their brown
diabetic patches. Her spine,
its milky yellow curve and, at the base,
one faded purple mole.

She lifts one breast and then the other
for me to dry. They have stretched over the years
to her stomach, the skin thinner
than rice paper.

The long veins

in each breast
are blue,
a surfacing blue
so clear it will take more
than a hundred years to forget.

# Li Qingzhao on Elegies

I do not want to be remembered.

Memory, you know, is a pathogen,
accumulating like microbes on an empty chair, between the ridges
on the sheets beside you.

I have spent my life with memories, little piles of words I thought to
manage. I have written elegies.

But
when I look again
each poem stands like a colossal statue
in a gallery of statues.

The crust of each face,
masked with its distant, archaic smile—
now falls away
and what returns is absence.

Outside, on jet-black soil,
I stand where I have planted rows.
In a week, their unintelligible leaves all pitch into the air.

# ACKNOWLEDGMENTS

Thank you to the editors of the following publications in which poems from this book first appeared:

*American Poets*: "They Sail Across the Mirrored Sea"

*Aquifer: The Florida Review Online*: "All Their Awful Particles"

*Cimarron Review*: "Fastened IV," "Fastened V"

*Ghost Proposal*: "Imago," "The Encounter," "Madame Butterfly at the Auction House," "In Which I Am Afflicted with Mme. Butterfly"

*Prodigal*: "Fastened III"

*Spillway*: "Fastened II"

*Tammy*: "It is a house," "Psalms"


Thank you to the Kimmel Harding Nelson Center for the Arts.

Heartfelt gratitude for my inspiring and generous teachers at Syracuse, particularly Mary Karr and Bruce Smith. My deepest appreciation and thanks to Brooks Haxton for his sharp eye and encouragement in all my endeavors. Thanks to my fellow writers in and out of workshops for their thoughtful critiques and friendships. Thanks also to Carlos Dorrien and Phyllis McGibbon for showing me what it means to live as an artist. To everyone at Tavern Books, thank you for making this book a reality. And lastly, thank you to my family and friends for their abundant kindness and love.

# TAVERN BOOKS

Tavern Books is a not-for-profit poetry publisher that exists to print, promote, and preserve works of literary vision, to foster a climate of cultural preservation, and to disseminate books in a way that benefits the reading public.

We publish books in translation from the world's finest poets, champion new works by innovative writers, and revive out-of-print classics. We keep our titles in print, honoring the cultural contract between publisher and author, as well as between publisher and public. Our catalog, known as The Living Library, sustains the visions of our authors, ensuring their voices remain alive in the social and artistic discourse of our modern era.

# ABOUT THE WROLSTAD CONTEMPORARY POETRY SERIES

To honor the life and work of Greta Wrolstad (1981-2005), author of *Night is Simply a Shadow* (2013) and *Notes on Sea & Shore* (2010), Tavern Books invites submissions of new poetry collections through the Wrolstad Contemporary Poetry Series during an annual reading period.

This series exists to champion exceptional literary works from young women poets through a book publication in The Living Library, the Tavern Books catalog of innovative poets ranging from first-time authors and neglected masters to Pulitzer Prize winners and Nobel Laureates. The Wrolstad Contemporary Poetry Series is open to any women aged 40 years or younger who is a US citizen, regardless of publication history.

For more information visit: tavernbooks.org/wrolstad-series

# SUBSCRIPTIONS

Become a subscriber and receive the next six Tavern Books titles at a substantial discount, delivered to your door. Paperback and hardcover subscriptions available.

For details visit www.tavernbooks.org/subscriptions or write to us at:

Tavern Books
at Union Station
800 NW 6th Avenue #255
Portland, Oregon 97209

# THE LIVING LIBRARY

*The Fire's Journey: Part IV* by Eunice Odio,
translated from the Spanish by Keith Ekiss
with Sonia P. Ticas and Mauricio Espinoza

*Full Body Pleasure Suit* by Elsbeth Pancrazi

*Duino Elegies* by Rainer Maria Rilke,
translated from the German by Gary Miranda

*Twelve Poems About Cavafy* by Yannis Ritsos,
translated from the Greek by Paul Merchant

*Monochords* by Yannis Ritsos,
translated from the Greek by Paul Merchant

*Glowing Enigmas* by Nelly Sachs,
translated from the German by Michael Hamburger

*Prodigy* by Charles Simic,
drawings by Charles Seluzicki

*Night of Shooting Stars* by Leonardo Sinisgalli,
translated from the Italian by W. S. Di Piero

*Skin* by Tone Škrjanec,
translated from the Slovene by Matthew Rohrer and Ana Pepelnik

*We Women* by Edith Södergran,
translated from the Swedish by Samuel Charters

*Winterward* by William Stafford

*Building the Barricade* by Anna Świrszczyńska,
translated from the Polish by Piotr Florczyk

*Baltics* by Tomas Tranströmer,
with photographs by Ann Charters,
translated from the Swedish by Samuel Charters

*For the Living and the Dead* by Tomas Tranströmer,
translated from the Swedish by John F. Deane

*Prison: Nine Haiku from Hällby Youth Prison* by Tomas Tranströmer,
translated from the Swedish by Malena Mörling

*Tomas Tranströmer's First Poems & Notes from the Land of Lap Fever*
by Tomas Tranströmer and Jonas Ellerström,
translated from the Swedish by Malena Mörling

*Collected Translations* by David Wevill

*Casual Ties* by David Wevill

*Where the Arrow Falls* by David Wevill

*A Christ of the Ice-Floes* by David Wevill

*Night Is Simply a Shadow* by Greta Wrolstad

*Notes on Sea & Shore* by Greta Wrolstad

*The Countries We Live In* by Natan Zach,
translated from the Hebrew by Peter Everwine

*\*forthcoming*

Tavern Books is funded, in part, by the generosity of philanthropic organizations, public and private institutions, and individual donors. By supporting Tavern Books and its mission, you enable us to publish the most exciting poets from around the world. To learn more about underwriting Tavern Books titles, please contact us by e-mail: info@tavernbooks.org.

## MAJOR FUNDING HAS BEEN PROVIDED BY

THE LIBRA FOUNDATION

## THE PUBLICATION OF THIS BOOK IS MADE POSSIBLE, IN PART, BY THE SUPPORT OF THE FOLLOWING INDIVIDUALS

Sophie Cabot Black
Audrey Block
Joe Bratcher
Dean & Karen Garyet
Daniel Handler
Kate Harbour
Ana Jokkmokk
Jennifer Jones & Mark Swartz
Leah Middlebrook
Joseph Millar & Dorianne Laux

Jay Ponteri
Mary Ann Ryan
Donna Swartz
Mary Szybist & Jerry Harp
Bill & Leah Stenson
Jonathan Wells
Dan Wieden
Wendy Willis & David Biespiel
Vince & Patty Wixon
Ron & Kathy Wrolstad

# COLOPHON

This book was designed and typeset by Eldon Potter at Bryan Potter Design, Portland, Oregon. Text is set in Garamond, an old-style serif typeface named for the punch-cutter Claude Garamond (c. 1480-1561). Display font is Futura, a modern classic of 1920s German design created by Paul Renner. True to its name, Futura continues to be unironically enlisted as an elegant and efficient typeface for display and text treatments, nearly 100 years later. *Unearthings* appears in both paperback and cloth-covered editions. Printed on archival-quality paper by McNaughton & Gunn, Inc.